RESPONSE

THE NATIONAL POETRY SERIES

The National Poetry Series was established in 1978 to publish five collections of poetry annually through five participating publishers. The manuscripts are selected by five poets of national reputation. Publication is funded by James A. Michener, The Copernicus Society of America, Edward J. Piszek, The Lannan Foundation, The National Endowment for the Arts, and the Tiny Tiger Foundation.

1995 COMPETITION WINNERS

Heather Allen, *Leaving a Shadow*
  Selected by Denise Levertov,
  published by Copper Canyon Press

Marcus Cafagna, *The Broken World*
  Selected by Yusef Komunyakaa,
  published by the University of Illinois Press

Daniel Hall, *Strange Relation*
  Selected by Mark Doty,
  published by Viking Penguin Press

Juliana Spahr, *Response*
  Selected by Lyn Hejinian,
  published by Sun & Moon Press

Karen Volkman, *Crash's Law*
  Selected by Heather McHugh,
  published by W. W. Norton

RESPONSE

Juliana Spahr

NEW AMERICAN POETRY
SERIES: 25

LOS ANGELES
SUN & MOON PRESS
1996

Sun & Moon Press
A Program of The Contemporary Arts Educational Project, Inc.
a nonprofit corporation
6026 Wilshire Boulevard, Los Angeles, California 90036

This edition first published in paperback in 1996 by Sun & Moon Press
10 9 8 7 6 5 4 3 2 1
FIRST EDITION
©1996 by Juliana Spahr
Biographical material ©1996 by Sun & Moon Press
All rights reserved

This book was made possible, in part, through support from
The National Poetry Series and through contributions to
The Contemporary Arts Educational Project, Inc.,
a nonprofit corporation

Some of these poems previously appeared in *Avec, Phoebe, The Iowa Review, Lingo,*
The Little Magazine and the chapbook *Testimony* (Meow Press).
The author wishes to thank the editors and publishers
of these magazines and presses.

Cover: Nam June Paik, *TV Buddah*, 1974 (Video installation with statue)
Design: Katie Messborn
Typography: Guy Bennett

LIBRARY OF CONGRESS CATALOGING IN PUBLICATION DATA
Spahr, Juliana.
Response / Juliana Spahr.—1st ed.
p. cm — (New American Poetry Series: 25)
ISBN: 1-55713-289-5 (alk. paper)
I. Title. II. Series.
PS3569.P3356R47   1996
811'.54—dc20
96-36730
CIP

Printed in the United States of America on acid-free paper.

contents

introduction

how to tell without violating?
how to approach mass thought patterns
> as history?
> as opportunity?
> as truth?
> as art?

the needles in coke bottles suddenly all over the nation
the sudden realization of being a Satanist
or a victim or a stalker of your self or an alien
> collaborator or an artist or a poet

psychoanalysis gone awry, some say
others, it is the fault of the mind

pleas are made:
"I am confused about what I believe or disbelieve. If I
believed or disbelieved what to be or not to be as I remem-
bered it or made it up or experienced it or dreamed it then
what else or nothing else about my past or my present is
true or false?"

aphorisms are formulated:
a lie goes better sandwiched between two truths
somewhere between the truth and the lie is the truth

often the plea is centered around the idea of self or other
        birthed thing
"I held my self (my child) and I satanically abused him or
her realized him or her to be half-other felt like she or he
was not my self (my child) but some other person's self
(child) "I held my self (child) and I was confused"
I held my self (child)

responding

This is a place without a terrain a government that always
 changes an unstable language. Even buildings disappear
 from day to day.

[gendered pronoun] wanders in this place
          [searching
            [waiting

the condition of unbearableness is the constant state of mind
 for all occupants

we read all day in the village square during the rule of [name
 of major historical figure] a book that is so subtle

      [its political content goes unnoticed

what is political content?

        [the question or the statement

[generic pronoun] creates

     [a reader culture

     [generic plural pronoun] prefer both

realism's authenticities are not the question

the question [role of art in the State

we know art is fundamental to the [New State] as is evidenced
    in village scenes, majestic ancient views, masses and
    masses of [generic human figures] marching in columns,
    swords coded as plowshares, image as spectacle

we know [name of city], [adjective], [name of major composer]
to recode [reduce] it: Linz, ambiguous, Wagner

we know [name of major historical figure] calls, authentically,
    for a more total, more radical war than we can even
    dream in the language of the avant-garde

we know a commercial promises to reduce plaque more
    effectively in this same tone

but sometimes we exceed even our own expectations to
    surprise even ourselves

something encloses the impossible in a fable

an unreal world called real because it is so heavily metaphoric

we can't keep our fingers of connection out of it

it is a ride in the country, the car crowded with children
                    [each child represents a different
                              ethnicity of [name of nation]

it is a moment of standing with light resonating around [major
      historical figure

it is a guiding of the child towards the right path

it is a picnic in a field, the spread is bountiful
[the spread of [name of nation] is represented through the
      arrangement of food on the checkered tablecloth

it is [name of major historical figure]'s Art Collection:
      figure after figure
      each carries spears, lunges, draws the arm back to pull
            tight the bow

      a ruined plaza has a [gendered human form] at its en
            trance

      a [generic child] draws a sword under the guidance of
      [generic possessive pronoun] [honorific denoting repro-
      ductive role]

a [generic human form] raises [generic pronoun] arms and
four horses turn away

another plays a lute

an eagle holds a symbol

fake [name of nation used as an adjective] heads

while the end of lunacy in art was explicit in [name of major
    historical figure]'s rhetoric

while when nation turns to art, art loses its divergence

while the [generic human figures] come back from war, their
    legs in fog

while a [generic human figure] sculpts, small against the
    expanse of marble, giving into the monumental human
    form that symbolizes eugenic possibilities

while another [generic human figure] pedantically draws
    postcards of village centers, operas, mountain vistas

while overwhelmed by an opera [name of major historical
    figure] plans genocide

III

we know we respond resistantly as faked children's books of
        realist adventure tales have turned into military instruc-
        tion manuals

or [name of major historical figure] hails a cab, [generic
        possessive human pronoun] hand raised here, beckoning
        as the red flag with [name of fast food chain] waves
        behind [generic human pronoun] and the red star on top
        of the [name of cultural landmark in major city] twinkles.

many people raise their hands for different purposes all day
        long

we are all always waiting for our cab to come

the question here is the same as that of a relationship
where does art define our vocabulary?

the margin declares

[it is impossible to speak about something

it is only possible to speak beside it

[a film with a voice-over of nonsense

to act in the unsecular forbidden margins [claims a certain
        privilege]

                        [generic human pronoun] cast a colonizing eye

a scripture of space / a place where

a [generic human form] twists in space
                                [follow this body]

getting you to recognize yourself in [generic possessive
        pronoun] work

                                [is kidnapping]

in the space of this question some emigrate or lapse into total
     silence

some co-opt this language and paint a series of meticulous and
     beautifully colored monumental images of people impris-
     oned and alone at the edge of a tedious despair

some [refigure [refuse] respond] call out for an end

rewritten, the goal of the artist is to prevent reality in a true and
     concrete manner

IV

[generic human figure] claims I can get more information at
     home than by going to the war scene

what [generic pronoun] sees is [gendered naked bodies] in
     news photos—dead bodies, discarded bodies, junk

I SAW THIS written on the bottom

                                        [a way of testimony

the poverty of image among the people of [name of nation]

the continual increase in the amount of image a viewer can
     tolerate

                              [who went to [name of nation?

returning again and again to images of torture

covert activities depicted   [blown up

                                              [to show power

                              details of photographs
                              or Xerox degradations
                              of photos on Duraclear
                              hang loose are
                              vulnerable and
                              fragmentary and
                              images are seen
                              through images and/or
                              viewers

[call this]
          the fate of Madame Bovery, the fate of Anna Karenina

a dog with a [generic human face] has slogans coming out
    of its mouth as angels hold its head back suckle at its
    tits

taped to a [gendered hand, adorned with ring] is a photo-
    graph of [gendered naked torso], gagged

[generic human figure] infects computerized images with
    digitized viruses and then transfers them to canvas with
    a robotic device

                    [possible responses to what is seen

in [name of nation] at another time another set of responses:

a [sexual category withheld] cuts hair and cameras circle
        around and [generic human pronoun] is dragged out of
        the room

another [generic human figure] says passionately we express
        ourselves in a language of regulations. Symbols and
        numbers best convey our ideas

another [generic human figure] makes an enormous painting
        of a massacre victim, mutilated and bloody, and hangs it
        by night on a pedestrian bridge

what a nation gives us is the image in [name of major weekly
        news source] of the [generic human figure] standing
        before the tanks with white flag

[generic pronoun] painted on houses, streets, stones, trees

[generic pronoun] covered [name of island] with strange marks
in chalk, oil paint, and dye

[generic pronoun] wished to reduce writing to the zero level
where it is without meaning. When culture invades
private life on a large scale [generic pronoun] said the
individual cannot escape being raped

another [generic noun] made a font that was scratched into
paper by a knife

this font made each letter into a single scratch

[generic pronoun] scratched the other [generic pronoun]'s
statement on rape into a banner and hung it outside

[my zero-level writing
[generic pronoun] said
                protest rape
[generic pronoun] said
my zero-level writing
[generic pronoun] said
dangerous cultural rape
[generic pronoun] said
my zero-level writing
my zero-level writing

v

a voice stutters in the background of our waking mind

[generic possessive pronoun] stutter is our stutter

or it is the way we define our difference?

stutter is nation

beneath an image of human figures the words [you have
nothing to lose but your chains

at times two voices talk to one another

[generic human] faces [tired]

we know we are all constructed

when it comes down to it we don't believe it

the social always holds us back

while the ways that we encounter relation are various

we remain

searching [searching

we question, respond

                                        [deny we [move forward

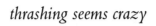
thrashing seems crazy

NOTE

This poem draws from an Oprah episode on the case of Ruth Finley, a woman who, because of "dissociative personality disorder," was stalked by a male persona of herself.

this is true
a man in an alley grabbed my arm
this is true
someone called me and left the phone dangling at the post office
this is true
a man stalked me

someone tells a story

someone tells a story to another person
another person says I don't believe this
someone tells the story again in an attempt to convince
someone tells

as disbelief is easy
belief is difficult, supported by constraint

but a woman knows a man stalked her
knows this is true

a woman knows her own address
her own body
her lost domain, her desires, her confusions

someone tells a story

there are things people can do to themselves
they are:
leave molotov cocktail on own yard
set fire to own house
leave a glass of urine on own porch
leave envelope of feces outside own door
send a butcher knife to self at work
send letter to health department that self is spreading v d
stab own back

someone tells this story
says this is true
self turns on self
the knife enters at a point that the self could not have reached
     but did
someone tells and then repeats and she stalks herself several
     times to convince
someone tries to enter into the information
to pass words back and forth that have meaning
fails, resorts to this is true

this is true
a woman calls her stalker The Poet

this is true
a woman describes a stalker in terms that describe herself

this is true
a woman stalked herself to kill herself

this is true
a woman is at times a man

when a fish is hooked
other fish don't see the hook

thrashing seems crazy

the hook could be the branding of a woman at a young age
        by a man
or an older male neighbor spending too much time with a
        child
or the boring nature of life

in the story the hook is the artist's rendering of the stalker as
        described by the woman
it is the woman in a man's face

she does not know this man
thrashing seems crazy

later she realizes it is herself
her knife
her hook
her own face she was always drawing male

this is true
as thrashing is not crazy when one is on the hook

documentary

in the narrative there are two men who killed the man they
thought was [name of nation used as an adjective deleted]
but who was really [name of nation used as an adjective
deleted]

two men said it could happen to everyone

a neighbor repeats this as if he had heard it before but replaces
everyone with anyone

killing is an ordinary act the two men, the neighbor, the
    numerous clips from news programs assure

the man who committed the murders comments on how
    the night he spent in jail, the next day was father's day,
    as if it mattered

[ordinary] has turned to all that is [injustice] [extraordinary]

[at] [a] [loss] [for] [words,]

in the narrative a man looking for an elevator door is
       metaphor for the causes that forced
[name of nation deleted] to become engulfed with looting,
       rioting, and dangerous uprising

this is a document
made of pieces scattered at [name of person made possessive
        deleted] feet

there is a huge hole in [name of nation deleted], a person says
a huge hole, a man killed, an unfound elevator door

we wait for the women carrying stones in their aprons to save
    [us] all
to beat down what is fearful in [name of nation deleted]

but 4/29 arrives before the women
carrying its many meanings

testimony

it often begins with a warning:

> The information in these papers should not be accepted in
> and of itself. You must seek out confirmation for yourself.
> The credibility of these papers does not depend on its author,
> but rather on what you discover from your study and investi-
> gation of the material presented.
>
> CONFIRM EVERYTHING FOR YOURSELF

this is about the role of testimony
the claims of truth in the age of cover-up and misinformation

people claim to have been abducted
claim to have been undressed and examined
poked and prodded
claim that there are complex reproductive enterprises involv-
    ing conception and gestation or incubation of mixed
    beings
claim they are caught up in these procedures
captured against their will
they claim mechanisms of ingestion and expulsion are exam-
    ined over and over
claim endless rounds of gynecological, rectal, and urologial
    procedures

and authorities report, a physiological exploitation accompa-
    nies these claims

or reason that because of the emphasis on reproduction
    women seem to have a larger number of complex
    experiences

or calculate that as many as one in ten Americans have im-
    plants as a result of these abductions

while others claim that electromagnetic symbols are used to
    control or trace people with implants

in the narrative she finds herself floating up and out of bed

through the window or screen or wall

she finds herself drawn towards the light and enveloped by it

she finds herself floating towards the light

in a preliminary investigation
they take a sharp instrument and scrape it down her soles,
     causing her feet to curl in reflex
they touch her ankles and twist her foot from side to side
they push and press against her calf muscles
they squeeze hard and painfully between the bone and calf
     muscle
they look closely at her knee and bend her leg a few times

but this is just the beginning and what follows this prodding
     remains difficult
twisted in its possible truth

mutilated claims
fetuses or the organs of elimination are missing
a woman who is carrying twins, for instance, might have one
       removed so only a single twin remains
or a fetus removed from a body by a sucking machine
or the rectal area perfectly cored out of a body found on the
       side of the road
or puncture wounds due to needles and probes on the head,
       the fingers, the leg

at other times instead of removal insertion, multiplication
one half being, one half human children

other reports vary
are disputed by the community of believers

a humanoid might have been housed at Los Alamos until its
      death in the early 1950s
a speech device which enabled the speaking of English might
      have been implanted in a throat
this being might have been named Ebe

a man devises a paranoid interpretation of what he thought he
      was seeing and hearing and begins to build a pyramid
      from his sources
his sources emphasize
a visiting being farms another being for organs, eats a being's
      flesh

photographs of sightings from afar often appear in grainy detail

the matter might have literally brought about the establishment
      of direct communication between the East and West in
      1962

whispers resonate: the church might refuse to take a stand
      because it would have to imagine God having a relation-
      ship with someone other than ourselves

in the midst of myth or belief
claims of an archetypal contact through symbology that begins
        fifty to one hundred years ago
the stories gain fluency, even as they present questions

there might be a book called the Bible which contains all these
        reports
the scrolls might be at the CIA headquarters in Langley,
        Virginia

but even the beings themselves deflect the subject's questions
     with palliatives and do not give substantive answers
in answer to the relentless question of "why?"
often they communicate only, "you know what you are
     doing"
or "you are very special to us"
or "this is very important and you are helping us"
at other times they give visualizations of planetary destruction
     and say "we will help you prevent this"

attempts at comfort from those without the vocabulary of
     comfort

III

testimony:

"this is a daily dose of pain"

                              "this is not a dream"
                    "I did not choose to join"
"I do not know why I keep waking"
            "I think I'm floating out a closed window"
"I wake up invaded"
                    "He puts something inside"
                              "I'm under something, it is a man"
      "and I'm saying 'this has to stop' over and over"
"They're pressing and there's snipping."
                        "It is just like Auschwitz, just like Auschwitz"
                "I have recurring nuclear war dreams"
              "Who analyzes like that? It's just something new"
"It is long and points. It is like a needle. It pinches"\
"They have an agenda to carry out and once it begins nothing
      can stop it"
                        "It can go on for years"
"I feel like this is psychological torture although I am not
      afraid for my life"
                              "Like possession in a way"

testimony:

"I can't say this happened to me and expect to be treated in the same way again"

"You have to go where the evidence leads you, even though you may not like going there"

"You can't say this happened to me and expect to be treated the same again"

"It forever changed the way I think about things"

"And I keep saying 'this has to stop,' 'this has to stop' and then suddenly I feel like all will be well"

"You go to where the UFO stories are"

testimony:

"they close our eyes"

"our voices are made silent"

"our ears are made deaf"

"we will never be the same again"

testimony:

"you will never be the same again"

"the alienness that you feel on your world is a reflection of the
        alienness you feel between each other"

"not alien but external
the boundaries of the world simply expanded"

testimony:

"nature abhors a vacuum
where a lack of openness
and a penchant for secrecy persists
rumor and rumors of rumor are sure to flourish
even in the middle of the desert

you keep shaking the secrecy tree
hopefully something drops out"

further complicating the flow of information: some documents
     are impossible to get
others disintegrate with five seconds exposure to air

these might tell of agreements between the US government
     and beings
perhaps granting beings permission to conduct animal mutila-
     tion

at other times, a man claims to be a source of false information
he might be sent by the government

another states "how do you know that I'm not here to either
     give you misinformation or to give you information
     which is part of the programming, knowing you are
     going to go out and spread it around?"
questions of truth are turned around, back to the sleuth in a
     beat up car who has given up his/her job to search for
     authenticity because this story is so big it will change the
     century

trust no one becomes an advertising slogan for the 90s

as the information here is suspect
a fraud will be enacted to prove other data is fraudulent
these fraudulent practices prove the truth of other data to some
        minds
(the fraud being evidence of the need to cover the truth)
others only remember the fraud
this creates a nightmare of violence and irrationality

at the end of every narrative are the "official response" and the
      "critic's corner"
or a series of questions for you the reader to answer:
why does s/he claim it was foggy when the weather bureau
      reported sun?
why are victims of sexual abuse more likely to be abducted
      than the general population?
why do the most convincing, most tantalizing sightings always
      have only one person to authenticate them?

v

my point here is not the laugh
nor the truth
nor to merely explore truth's turns, information's conspiracies

it is:

what do we do?

trust no one?

trust no I?

as we try to look with eyes better than what we've had before

what does it mean to believe oneself as attractive to an alien
     race?

a life defined by questions

was I abducted?

did I experience that or just remember it?

                         never to be answering

                         stuttering one's way through
                              the unreliability of hypnosis

claim for us it is not the proof but the telling

spots on film
charred grass
pieces of metal

all begin to mean in new ways

as there is the possibility that beings might have hired a PR firm
    which created *My Favorite Martian, ALF, Star Trek, Star*
    Wars, AlienNation, ET, and other shows post the 1950s
all media become evidence or proof
or part of the conspiracy to expose beings

we will become used to visiting beings, welcome them on the
    basis of this entertainment exposure

so the boy running off into the field, clouds rolling over head,
    is called
calling out to us

so the call to phone home
so the force
so the FBI is covering up
so the aliens are the minority

entertainment takes a larger purpose
one ominous or liberating

the breadth of the debate

as we rethink our selves, the political enters
and the issue twists to become about our ability to touch
        information
to make our own decisions
which has been required of us all along, we've just slacked off
letting the advertisement speak a larger truth
letting others do our thinking and condense it back to us as a
        series of dialectical issues

our lives were busy, we defend our laziness
filled with the everyday, never out of the ordinary

so what interests in this formula are the questions without
        answers
which lie to believe
becomes the question
is it the liar or the truth-teller encountered at the crossroads,
        pointing the direction

the direction amphibious

more than identity our attraction is to puzzle
the lineage of close encounters
anecdotal data, exhaust residue, radiation levels five times the
        norm

witness

I

when terrible things happen they must be witnessed

II

The narrative begins when the person walks into an office to give blood. The arm that is handed over is frail. A rubber tube is tied around this arm by a nurse. The arm gradually goes numb. The person orders the nurse: talk to me. The nurse talks about what s/he is doing. S/he says this rubber tubing will build up the pressure in your arm, will isolate your blood, will allow the removal of a limited amount of blood. The needle pricks the person's arm. Two vials of blood are filled. The blood is deep red. It contains within it the information that will provide witness.

III

in a world like this everything becomes about witness or cure

things that once meant nonsense now carry meaning

witness attempts to give meaning to *this*

attempts to step towards the beginning place
to move to cure
to move to action

but as always questions remain

when does witness no longer witness?

when does faith turn to act?

why is everything reduced to letters, to abbreviations?

how does one write the question of letters and not appropriate
    or make bland?

so there are reminders to think about the witness

to take responsibility for the feelings of the witness

for your witnessing

your moment of looking

not to fetter and feel for the sake of witness

but to add to look to this equation

the boundaries and limits of what is said by both the ill and
    the well expanded

attempts at witnessing:

a person waits in a darkening room for a phone call

a person sits in a hospital bed watching television

a person waits for a ride at the street corner

a person has a dream and discounts its validity

a car arrives and picks up a person after a conversation at a
    window

a person agrees to have sex with another person in the back of
    a car on a deserted road

all the while:

a person turns to another person and says: they were unable
    to stop the bleeding

a person gets an infusion of liquid through an iv

a person gets shot after shot, takes pill after pill

v

questions continue:

what are expressions?

what are experiences?

what are outcomes?

how much self can be removed and the self remain?

in the case of blood, witness is charting

these charts might be held on clipboards, hung at the end of
    the bed
might be submitted to the court
might be discussed in a run down health services office

witness: I finally got tested and felt relief but still fear for the
    future

Theresa Hak Kyung Cha writes of witnessing the Japanese
    occupation of Korea

she writes: unfathomable, the words, the terminology.

her list: enemy, atrocities, conquest, betrayal, invasion,
    destruction

here is the beginning of another list from another invasion:
    blood, semen, breast milk, vaginal fluid intermittent or
    persistent fever, fatigue, weakness, diarrhea, malaise,
    weight loss, lymphadenopathy

I saw this:

on the wall of a building a person has drawn a face
it is drawn in memorium
this face represents the other names written on a door in the
     wall
the names are:
Gloria Ed Junior Ken 8Ball Diamond Tony S Lou 8Str Emily
     June B Pito Jose Dave Ben Oscar Wally Chloe Hector
     Andy Carlos Gringo Jr. Ralphy TSP HTC BBP TOB
     George Daddy Pocholo

other names—Joni Sloth Janet Jeff—are written in others'
     scripts,
graffiti added to the wall of graffiti

this list continues to change over time

this is to bear witness

to make memorium

to have remembrance of what is dead

because there is little information distributed by the system and
        its institutions
other forms of information appear

a person says I am a teenager and I give you information
a person gives a talk before a group of people
a person brings bleach around to clean needles
a person drops off books everyday at various bars on his/her
        way home from work

these instruct in forms of protection
the drawings that accompany this form of witness are simply
        lined, pornographic
 abstinence is not really given much credence

instead language is explicit

it says:
get it on

it says
that dick has to be hard before you put a condom on it

it says
if the penis is uncut (uncircumcised), pull the foreskin back
        first

it says

for anal intercourse, use lots of lube. Lube is great for vaginal
intercourse, too

it says

guys—if you cum in the condom while having sex, hold the
condom near your balls and pull out while you're still
hard

the language of this discourse is a marriage of scientific terms,
        personal observation, and pornography
it is often detached and without anger

but there is another sort of discourse that adds anger
people yell at congresspeople as they enter their workplace
people stage die-ins
people carry signs and scream
people shut down churches, march in parades, carry banners
        where not wanted

the anger is to draw attention to the way anger is a just re-
        sponse
to how they will be angry until just witness is begun

"I've seen this:"

s/he screams
s/he screams in the office of his/her representative
s/he screams at this representative's assistant

the futility of screaming at the assistant well represents the
        futile necessity of anger

the assistant is angry at first
angry at the screaming
angry back
screaming back

then the assistant realizes
all s/he has to do is call the guards
and the problem goes away

s/he calls the guards
they come and the problem goes away

the witness of speech:

"I took his/her hand in mine and I cried."

"I asked to be left alone with my disabling sense of time."

"I begged everyone I knew to assist when the time came."

"S/he kept asking and asking why is this happening to us, to me."

an attempt to speak to the human moment will occur
in these moments someone touches someone
someone claims to love someone
someone moves closer to someone in prelude to a proposition
someone waits outside for someone to come by
someone becomes unable to live his/her life and succumbs

this is information that might be left out of witness
yet it has a bearing that is all the more strong

it speaks to the safety of immunity that does not exist
to the various other kinds of immunity that do exist
such as an emotional immunity to the world
a quarantine of engagement
a feeling of safety

which one do you believe?

just as a group of people join a cult of safe sex another group is
        formed that refuses to do so
this group might be teenagers or adults or women or men
this second group of people might feel that death is part of any
        act and accept the risks
or they might just be naive or feel bullied

people from the first group often join the second group at
        various points in their lives

and vice versa

people often lie about which group they belong to at any
        given moment

which group one belongs to on any given night might involve
        a highly elaborate struggle of power that depends on who
        is dominant, who loves, who is lost, who is drunk or
        stoned, who feels safe, who feels unsafe, who cares, who
        doesn't care

these struggles are endlessly variable and unchartable

they are absent from the rhetoric that is a marriage of scientific
        terms, personal observation, and pornography

they are moments that are impossible to witness
yet they are the moments that are so much a part of the
    everyday
of everyone's day or night
so they become some of the most important moments
and they are beyond the boundaries and limits of what is
    said by both the ill and the well

IX

in a world without hope, there is only hope

in a place of disease, there is only hope

in a time of trouble, the song instructs, turn to me

who is me?

x

turn on the lights
one person urges another person
turn on the lights

For a complete list of our poetry publications
write us at Sun & Moon Press
6026 Wilshire Boulevard
Los Angeles, California 90036